When Brother Fought Brother: THE American Civil War

By Carole Marsh

Editor:
Chad Beard

Cover Design:
Victoria DeJoy

Design & Layout:
Cecil Anderson
Lynette Rowe

Gallopade is proud to be a member of these educational organizations and associations:

The National School Supply and Equipment Association (NSSEA)
National Association for Gifted Children (NAGC)
American Booksellers Association (ABA)
Association of Partners for Public Lands (APPL)
Museum Store Association (MSA)
Publishers Marketing Association (PMA)
International Reading Association (IRA)

Published by

GALLOPADE™
INTERNATIONAL

800-536-2GET
www.gallopade.com

CAROLE MARSH BOOKS

Other Carole Marsh Books

Orville & Wilbur Wright . . . Step Out Into The Sky!
Lewis & Clark Go On a Hike: The Story of the Corps of Discovery
"What A Deal!": The Louisiana Purchase
How Our Nation Was Born: The American Revolution
When Brother Fought Brother: The American Civil War
The Fight For Equality: The U.S. Civil Rights Movement

State Stuff™, Available for all 50 states:

My First Pocket Guide
State My First Book
State Wheel of Fortune Gamebook
State Survivor Gamebook
State Illustrated Timelines
"Jography!": A Fun Run Through Our State

The State Coloring Book
The Big Reproducible Activity Book
State Millionaire Gamebook
State Project Books
Jeopardy: Answers & Questions About
    Our State

1,000 Readers™

Orville and Wilbur Wright
Louisiana Purchase
Benjamin Franklin
Martin Luther King, Jr

Meriwether Lewis & William Clark
George Washington
Ulysses S. Grant
Rosa Parks

Sacagawea
Paul Revere
Robert E. Lee
Thurgood Marshall

Patriotic Favorites™

Patriotic Favorites Coloring Book
Patriotic Biographies
The Daily Patriot: 365 Quotations

Young Patriots Coloring & Activity Book
Patriotic Projects
Patriotism: 365 Definitions

Table of Contents

A Word From the Author

Dear reader,

A civil war is a tragic thing. We read about them in the world headlines of our daily newspapers. Once, America had her very own Civil War! The new family of states was trying to settle down and learn how to live together as a country; it was more difficult than they had anticipated.

Despite being busy with new repsonsibilities and opportunities, Americans grew distracted over the issue of slavery. The country became divided between people for slavery and those against slavery.

In 1860, Abraham Lincoln was elected president of the United States. He was against slavery. Farmers in southern states, who relied on slave labor to run their plantations, did not want the federal government to end, or even limit, their "right" to own slaves.

Because they believed that their rights were being threatened, Southern states began to secede, or break away, from the Union. Shortly after, the Civil War began.

I hope that you have as much fun learning about the Civil War as I had writing this book. I think you will find that there are a lot of interesting and true facts about this time in our nation's history.

Carole Marsh

A Timeline of Events

November 6, 1860 – Abraham Lincoln is elected president.

December 1860 – South Carolina secedes from the Union followed by Mississippi, Florida, Alabama, Georgia, Louisiana, and Texas.

February 9, 1861 – The Confederate States of America is formed with Jefferson Davis, a West Point graduate and former U.S. Army officer, as president.

April 12, 1861 – Confederates attack Fort Sumter in Charleston, South Carolina. The Civil War begins.

April 1861 – Virginia secedes from the Union, followed by Arkansas, Tennessee, and North Carolina, forming an eleven-state Confederacy.

September 17, 1862 – The bloodiest day in U.S. military history as Confederate Armies are stopped at Antietam in Maryland. By nightfall 26,000 men are dead, wounded, or missing.

September 22, 1862 – President Lincoln issues the Emancipation Proclamation freeing all slaves in territories held by Confederates and emphasizes the enlisting of black soldiers in the Union Army.

March 3, 1863 – The U.S. Congress enacts a draft affecting male citizens aged 20-45.

July 1-3, 1863 – The tide of war turns against the South, as the Confederates are defeated at the Battle of Gettysburg in Pennsylvania.

November 19, 1863 – President Lincoln delivers a two-minute Gettysburg Address at a ceremony dedicating the Battlefield as a National Cemetery.

December 21, 1864 – Sherman reaches Savannah in Georgia leaving behind a 300-mile long path of destruction 60 miles wide all the way from Atlanta.

April 9, 1865 – Robert E. Lee surrenders his Confederate Army to Ulysses S. Grant at the village of Appomattox Court House in Virginia.

April 14, 1865 – John Wilkes Booth shoots President Lincoln.

December 6, 1865 – The Thirteenth Amendment to the United States Constitution, passed by Congress on January 31, 1865, is ratified. Slavery is abolished.

When Brother Fought Brother:
THE American Civil War

In April 1861, the American Civil War began. Four long years later, the war that pitted brother against brother was finally finished. In between, more than 620,000 Americans died, with disease killing twice as many as those killed in battle. About 50,000 survivors returned home as amputees. More than 4 million slaves gained their freedom.

The United States lost a president, was torn in two, and was finally put back together again. This is the story of the American Civil War.

How Can War Be Civil?

How can war be *civil*? Since the days of the American Civil War, this question has been asked. The two words together seem like an oxymoron. The word *civil* has two meanings. First of all, it can mean *polite* in a way that is very formal. However, it also can mean to have to do with what happens within a country. One might refer to a good citizen as a *civil* servant.

The phrase *civil war* means a war within a country. There are civil wars happening right now in different countries around the world. The American Civil War was not the first civil war either. England had its own civil war from about 1640–1660.

Southerners called it...

- The War Between the States
- Mr. Lincoln's War
- The War of Southern Independence
- The War in Defense of Virginia
- The War of Northern Aggression

Northerners called it...

- The War of the Rebellion
- The War of Southern Rebellion
- The War to Save the Union
- The War for Abolition

Unscramble the letters below to find out another name for the American Civil War.

WORD DEFINITION

oxymoron: two words together that have opposite meanings — like freezer burn

heT aWr etweben teh tateSs

___ ___ ___   ___ ___ ___   ___ ___ ___ ___ ___ ___ ___

___ ___ ___   ___ ___ ___ ___ ___ ___

North Vs. South

At the time of the Civil War, the North and South had different economies. The economy in the northern part of the United States was industrialized. The economy of the Southern part of the United States was agricultural and relied on slave labor.

Label the scenes representing the economy of the North with an "N." Label the scenes representing the economy of the South with an "S."

1 _____

2 _____

3 _____

5 _____

4 _____

The Civil War was the North versus South, right? Yes, but war is not quite that simple. There were some Northerners who believed in states' rights! There were some Southerners who were opposed to slavery!

A Nation Divided

The West was beginning to open up for new settlement. Many territorial leaders dreamt of statehood. The question was whether or not these states would be slave states or free states?

Southern states felt threatened. If there were more free states than slave states, Southerners feared that slavery would be abolished. That would mean disaster for Southern economies!

Northerners also felt threatened. Businesses could make more money using slave labor than paying for workers. Working-class families would not be able to make a living in new states if slavery was allowed.

After looking at the map, answer the questions below!

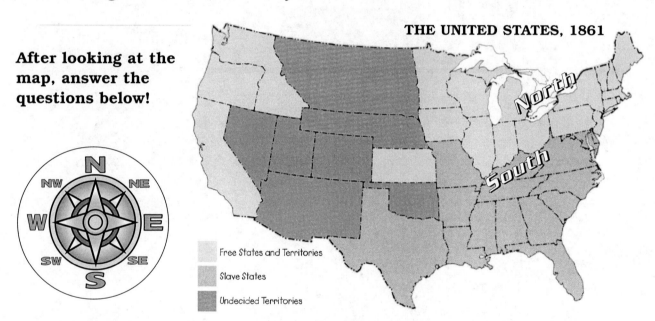

THE UNITED STATES, 1861

Free States and Territories

Slave States

Undecided Territories

1. Which states on the map were in favor of slavery and secession?
2. Which states were in favor of abolition and preserving the Union?
3. How many undecided territories were there in 1861?
4. How many free states and Territories were there in 1861?
5. How many slave states were there in 1861?

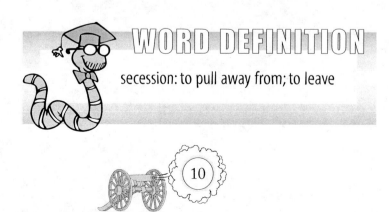

WORD DEFINITION

secession: to pull away from; to leave

Slavery Has Got to Go!

People who tried to get rid of slavery were called abolitionists. They began their fight against slavery years before the Civil War began. Abolitionists wanted to see slaves go free. They campaigned to end slavery. They brought national attention to the abolitionist movement. Many of them broke the law at the time for what they believed was right. Some lost their lives so that others might have a chance for freedom.

Match the abolitionist leader with his or her description.

____ 1. Nat Turner

____ 2. John Brown

____ 3. Harriet Tubman

____ 4. Frederick Douglass

____ 5. Harriet Beecher Stowe

____ 6. William Lloyd Garrison

____ 7. Sojourner Truth

____ 8. John Greenleaf Whittier

A. Famous abolitionist poet from New England

B. Led a raid on the U.S. Armory at Harper's Ferry, Virginia (present-day West Virginia)

C. Became the most famous leader of the Underground Railroad

D. Led a revolt against plantation owners in Virginia

E. Former slave who became a famous public speaker

F. Author of antislavery novel, *Uncle Tom's Cabin*

G. Isabella Baumfree changed her name to match her goals

H. Published abolitionist newspaper, *The Liberator*

I'm a member of the Bugs of the Confederacy!

I'm a Yankee Doodle Bug!

Lincoln For President!

In 1860, Abraham Lincoln was elected president of the United States. Lincoln was against slavery. By the time he actually took office, seven southern states had seceded from the Union. They not only wanted to preserve the institution of slavery, but also wanted the right to make their own laws without interference from the federal government.

These states formed a separate government. They called this government the Confederate States of America. Lincoln insisted that secession was illegal. He swore that he would protect federal possessions located in the South.

In December 1860, South Carolina seceded from the Union. Within a few weeks, Mississippi, Florida, Alabama, Georgia, Louisiana, and Texas also seceded. In April 1861, Virginia seceded from the Union. Later that year, Arkansas, Tennessee, and North Carolina also seceded forming an eleven-state Confederacy.

BORDER STATES:

Missouri and Kentucky did not secede from the Union, but secessionists within each state sent representatives to the Confederate Congress. This accounts for the 13 stars in the Confederate flag even though only 11 states actually joined the Confederacy.

Use a red crayon to color each of the states that seceded from the Union.

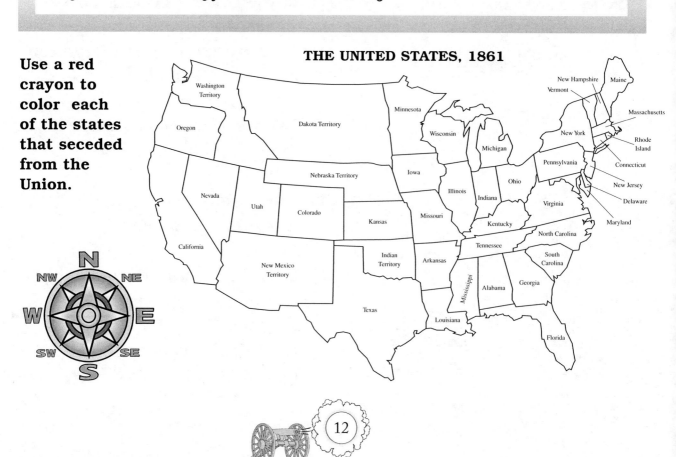

THE UNITED STATES, 1861

Fort Sumter Surrenders

Fort Sumter was the site of the first shot fired in the American Civil War. On April 12, 1861, Confederate forces fired on the fort, which stood on an island in the harbor of Charleston, South Carolina. The following day, after heavy bombing, United States troops surrendered to Confederate forces. On April 14, the U.S. troops withdrew from the fort. Not a single person was killed in the battle.

Fort Sumter had been a symbol for both the North and the South since December 1860, when South Carolina became the first Southern State to secede from the Union. The crisis reached its peak when President Abraham Lincoln ordered that supplies be sent to the fort. Confederates chose to fire on the fort rather than allow it to be resupplied.

Make your own Fort Sumter flag!

The United States flag that flew over Fort Sumter in 1861 was different than the U.S. flag Americans use today. There were thirteen stripes, but there were only 33 stars (one for each state). **Make your own Fort Sumter flag by following these instructions.**

❶ Use the pattern to cut stars from white construction paper.

❷ Cut seven strips of red construction paper.

❸ Cut a rectangle from blue construction paper.

❹ Attach blue rectangle, white stars, and red stripes to a large, rectangular piece of white construction paper using glue or tape.

❺ Proudly display the Fort Sumter Flag.

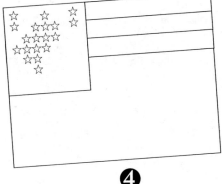

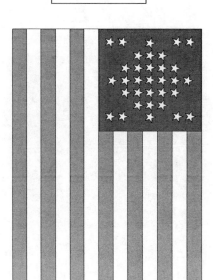

War Is No Picnic!: July 21, 1861

The first major battle of the Civil War was fought at Manassas, Virginia, not far from Washington, near a muddy stream known as Bull Run. Everyone in Washington and the surrounding area had heard talk of the troops gathering outside of town. Many citizens expected that the Union troops would quickly defeat their Confederate brothers. Buggies full of spectators traveled the thirty miles from Washington to see the battle. Picnic baskets were opened and folks prepared to watch the show. It didn't take long for people to realize that war is no picnic!

The reality of the battlefield was torn limbs, dying screams, and the living picking the pockets of the dead. By afternoon it was no longer entertaining — the battle became terrifying! Bodies littered the ground, the earth was bloody and beginning to smell, and neither side seemed to be winning. Then fresh Southern troops arrived. The Rebels attacked with bloodcurdling shouts they called the "rebel yell." The South won the first battle of Bull Run.

U.S. CIVIL WAR STATISTICS

	Killed	Wounded	Captured/Missing
Confederate	387	1,582	13
Union	460	1,124	1,312

Do the Math!

1. How many more Union soldiers were captured or missing after the battle? _____

2. How many more Union troops were killed during the battle? _____

3. How many more Confederate troops were wounded? _____

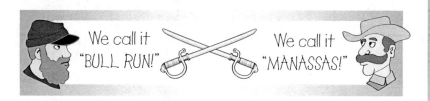

We call it "BULL RUN!"

We call it "MANASSAS!"

General Thomas Jackson was so brave at the first Battle of Bull Run (Manassas) that he was compared to a "stone wall." That is how he got his nickname, "Stonewall" Jackson.

Hey Sawbones!

By the end of the Civil War, disease had killed two soldiers for every one that was killed on the battlefield. Many soldiers did not understand that garbage and waste should be kept away from their drinking supply. Wounded soldiers stayed in "hospitals" that used to be cow-houses, wagon-sheds, hay-barracks, hen-coops, and barns. Soldiers often hid minor wounds for fear they would die if they went to a hospital.

Amputation was often used as a treatment for unrepairable or infected wounds. A wound to the arms or legs was fixed with amputation. There was little that surgeons could do to help a soldier with a wound to the stomach. Upon entering an army field hospital, it was not uncommon to see a pile of human fingers, feet, legs, and arms at the door. About 50,000 survivors returned home as amputees.

Doctors did not know about germs during the Civil War. Surgeons might wipe off their bonesaw with a cloth or rinse it in a tub of cold bloody water, then continue to the next patient. Civil War surgeons often used a bonesaw. Soldiers began to call doctors "sawbones" which became a nickname for doctors.

Soap Crayons

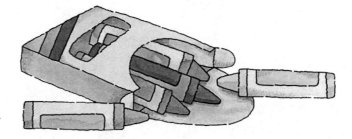

Makes: 20 Crayons

Ingredients:
- 1 cup soap flakes
- food coloring
- 2 tablespoons hot water

1. Have one large bowl and several small bowls, one for each color. You will also need an ice cube tray with different sections, or containers.

2. Put soap flakes in a large bowl and pour the hot water into the soap flakes, stirring constantly. The mixture will be extremely thick and hard to stir.

3. Spoon some of the soap into each of the small bowls and color each separately, adding the color by drops until the soap has the consistency of a very thick paste.

4. Press spoonfuls of the soap into your molds and set the crayons in a dry place to harden. They should take a few days to a week to dry completely. When dry, remove from the molds and allow to dry for a few more days before using.

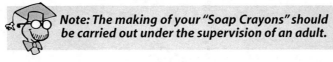

Note: The making of your "Soap Crayons" should be carried out under the supervision of an adult.

Hungry for Hardtack?

When a soldier was in camp, he usually ate pretty well, but the food was not very exciting. It usually was very plain. Soldiers ate dried beef or bacon, beans or peas, bread, and coffee. The officers enjoyed better food. Some of them even brought their own personal servants or cooks to war with them.

When the army was on the move, each soldier carried hardtack, salt pork, coffee, and a little sugar and salt. To improve their diet, soldiers often lived off the land, looking for wild berries or game. Soldiers bought (and sometimes stole) crops and animals from farms.

Make Your Own Hardtack

During the 1800s, hardtack was a common food for sailors and pioneers heading west. Civil War soldiers often ate it because it was easy for them to make in camp. It was pretty plain though, so you might want to enjoy your hardtack with jam or syrup.

Homemade Hardtack

Ingredients:
- 5 cups unbleached, all purpose flour
- 1 tablespoon salt
- 1 to 1 1/2 cups water

Cut out

To prepare:
Preheat oven to 450 degrees Fahrenheit

1. Combine flour and salt.
2. Add water until you can form a firm ball. If the dough gets sticky, add more flour. If it gets too dry, add more water.
3. Roll out on a well-floured surface, using liberal amounts of flour to keep dough from sticking to roller. Roll to approximately 1/2 inch thickness.
4. Cut dough into squares and poke with holes.
5. Place on cookie sheet and put into preheated oven. Bake for 20 minutes (until lightly browned).

Cut out

Note: The preparation of this dish should be carried out under the supervision of an adult.

Where is the Mason-Dixon Line?

The Mason-Dixon Line is usually thought of as the line that divides the North and the South. Before the Civil War, the southern boundary of Pennsylvania was considered the dividing line between slave states and free states. The Mason-Dixon line actually is the boundary line that separates Pennsylvania from Maryland and part of West Virginia, and the boundary between Maryland and Delaware.

Maryland was a slave state, and it was south of the Mason-Dixon Line. However, Maryland remained in the Union. After Virginia joined the Confederacy, the fate of Washington, D.C., depended on whether Maryland remained in the Union. If Maryland joined the Confederacy, Washington, D.C., would be surrounded by Confederate territory. Abraham Lincoln called for Union forces to rush across Maryland to defend the nation's capital. Although Maryland remained in the Union, many Marylanders joined the Confederate armies.

Connect the dots to find the path of the Mason-Dixon Line.

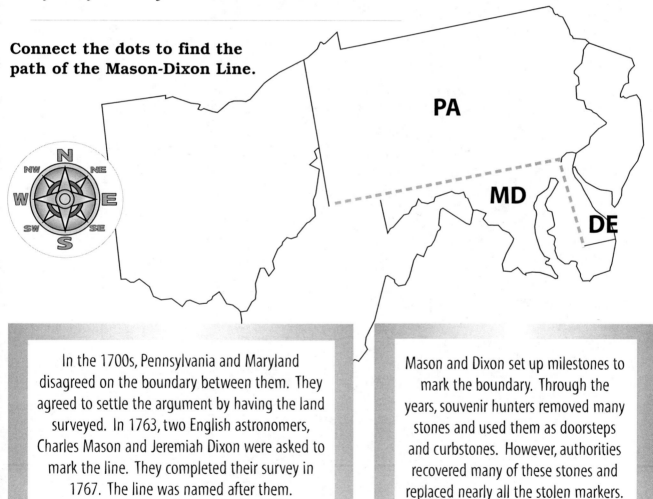

In the 1700s, Pennsylvania and Maryland disagreed on the boundary between them. They agreed to settle the argument by having the land surveyed. In 1763, two English astronomers, Charles Mason and Jeremiah Dixon were asked to mark the line. They completed their survey in 1767. The line was named after them.

Mason and Dixon set up milestones to mark the boundary. Through the years, souvenir hunters removed many stones and used them as doorsteps and curbstones. However, authorities recovered many of these stones and replaced nearly all the stolen markers.

17

Battle of the Ironclads: March 8, 1862

On March 8, 1862, the Confederate ironclad ship named the *Merrimack* sank two Union ships near Hampton Roads, Virginia, and ran three others aground. The *Merrimack* returned the next day to finish the job, but it found a Union ironclad, the *Monitor*, waiting. What followed was the first battle between ironclad warships.

The two ships battled for more than three hours. However, their bullets had little effect on each other, and the battle ended in a draw. Within a year, both ships were lost. The *Merrimack* was destroyed to keep it from being captured by the Union. The *Monitor* filled with water and sank while being towed at sea in a storm.

The *Merrimack* (sometimes spelled *Merrimac*) originally was a wooden ship. After the Civil War began, Union troops sank it when they evacuated the Navy yard at Portsmouth, Virginia. Confederate forces raised the ship and covered it with iron plates. They renamed it *Virginia*, though it is often referred to by its original name.

C.S.S. stands for Confederate States ship.

U.S.S. stands for United States ship.

Women in the Civil War

Many women stayed home while their husbands, brothers, and sons went off to fight the war. However, at least 3,200 women served as paid nurses, mostly for the North. Several hundred more posed as men and enlisted. In some cases, women who served as soldiers refused to get medical help from doctors for fear their secret would be discovered.

Women in the North and the South also had to fight for jobs. Many factories did not pay a fair wage and there were often not enough jobs to go around. Many women in the North went on strike to win higher paying jobs. In the South, women often had to struggle to find enough food to feed their children and themselves.

The Angel of the Battlefields

During the Civil War, one woman in particular became well known for her efforts to help others. She was Clara Barton. She collected supplies and took them to the battlefields. She also nursed injured soldiers. She was nicknamed "the angel of the battlefields."

Clara Barton went on to set up the American Red Cross in 1881. She and co-workers brought food and supplies to areas where disasters took place. She directed the American Red Cross until 1904. Today, this organization still takes care of those who need help the most.

Food in the South became scarce. Flour and other goods were sometimes priced unfairly. In Salisbury, North Carolina, dozens of women used axes to smash stores and then carted away 20 barrels of flour — the price of flour soon dropped!

Dorothea Dix was the Superintendent of Women Nurses for the Union side in the Civil War, but she is most famous for her work with the mentally ill. She brought about many changes in the treatment for the insane as well as the condition of jails in the United States and Europe.

Flags of the Civil War: North

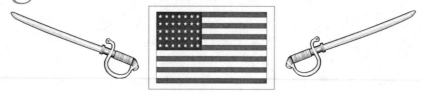

Union Flags

The United States had several different national flags during the Civil War. Though similar, they each were different in one very special way — the number of stars! Since 1818, an act of Congress calls for 13 stripes and one star for each state, to be added to the flag on the 4th of July following the admission of each new state. However, the act did not say how the stars should be arranged. For many years, the stars were arranged in different patterns on every flag! The U.S. flag is often called the "Stars and Stripes."

When the Civil War began, there were thirty-three stars representing the thirty-three states. Kansas was admitted to the Union on January 29, 1861, and a thirty-fourth star was added to the flag on July 4, 1861.

In 1863, Virginians were divided over secession from the Union, which led to the creation of West Virginia. Conflicts arose between the eastern counties that relied on slavery and the western counties that favored the abolition of slavery. West Virginia was admitted to the Union as the 35th state on June 20, 1863. A thirty-fifth star was added on July 4, 1864.

Nevada joined the Union October 31, 1864. Its nickname is the "Battle-born State" because it joined the Union during the Civil War. A thirty-sixth star was added to the flag on July 4, 1865, a few months after the Civil War was over.

During the Civil War, some members of Congress wanted to take stars away from the flag to represent the Confederate States leaving the Union. President Lincoln believed that the Southern states were still part of the Union and the stars were not taken away.

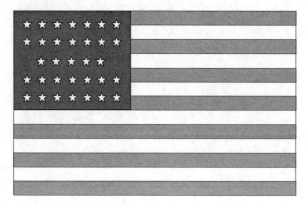

THE 33-STAR FLAG
(1859-1861)

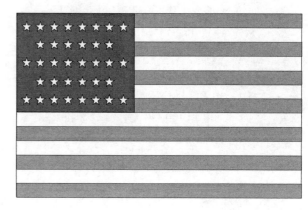

THE 36-STAR FLAG
(1865-1867)

Flags of the Civil War: South

Confederate Flags

The first flag of the Confederate States of America, called the "Stars and Bars," was approved by the Congress of the Confederate States, and first raised over the capitol building in Montgomery, Alabama on March 4, 1861. There would have been 7 stars from March 4, 1861 until May 7, 1861, when Virginia became the eighth Confederate State. Another star was to be added each time a state joined the Confederacy. Southerners were proud of their American roots and many of them liked the red, white, and blue colors of the "Stars and Stripes."

As the Civil War continued, Confederate soldiers complained that the "Stars and Bars" was too much like the "Stars and Stripes" of the Union. Reports that soldiers killed their own troops in the confusion of battle caused Confederate leaders to design a new flag. This flag was called the "Stainless Banner." It incorporated a Confederate battle flag used by many Southern regiments, but the flag was mostly white. This flag was approved by President Jefferson Davis on May 1, 1863.

When the "Stainless Banner" was used during battle, it sometimes looked like a plain white flag of surrender. The Confederate Congress decided to add a red stripe on the end of the "Stainless Banner." The last flag of the Confederacy was approved by President Jefferson Davis on March 4, 1865, four years to the day after the first raising of the "Stars and Bars" in Montgomery. The Civil War ended a little more than a month later.

"Bonnie Blue"
This flag was first seen being carried through the crowd of the convention when Mississippi decided to secede from the union. It stands primarily for unity.

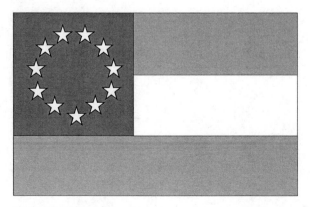

FIRST NATIONAL
FLAG (1861-1863)

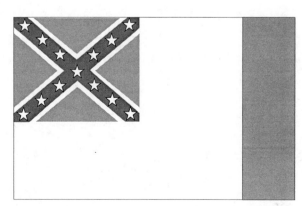

THIRD NATIONAL
FLAG (1865)

The Bloodiest Battle of the Civil War: September 17, 1862

The bloodiest battle of the Civil War occurred between Antietam Creek and the town of Sharpsburg, Maryland. It was the first major Civil War battle on Northern soil. More than 26,000 men were killed, wounded, or went missing in a single day. More soldiers were killed and wounded than the deaths of all Americans in the Revolutionary War, War of 1812, Mexican War, and Spanish-American War combined.

THE "BLOODIEST BATTLE" STATISTICS

	Killed	Wounded	Captured/Missing
Confederate	2,700	9,024	2,000
Union	2,108	9,549	753

Do the Math!

1. How many more Confederate soldiers were captured or missing after the battle? _____

2. How many more Confederate troops were killed during the battle? _____

3. How many more Union troops were wounded? _____

4. How many soldiers were killed altogether? _____

5. How many soldiers were wounded altogether? _____

Union General Ambrose Burnside is now best known for having lent his name to the distinctive side whiskers he wore — "burnsides" having been turned into "sideburns."

We call it "ANTIETAM!"   We call it "SHARPSBURG!"

22

African Americans in the Civil War

North

At the beginning of the Civil War, there was a law which said that "nonwhites" could not serve in the U.S. Army. Black militia-regiments of freedmen from Louisiana were turned away when they offered their services to Federal troops. However, there was no such law regarding the Navy. Eventually the laws were changed, and many African Americans did serve in the Union Army and Navy. Some African American soldiers stayed in the Army after the war. Troops in the West were nicknamed "Buffalo Soldiers."

"The 54th"

The first black regiment from the North was the 54th Massachusetts Infantry. The bravery of this group opened the door for 179,000 other black troops who eventually served in the Union.

South

Confederate Armies used African American slaves and freedmen as laborers. Many freedmen who lived in the South served in the Union Army or Navy. It may not have been legal, but there were some slaves who showed up on muster roles. Jacob Jones, a musician with the 9th Virginia, for example. Three freedmen served aboard the C.S.S. *Chicora*.

On March 13, 1865, President Jefferson Davis signed into law a bill passed by Congress calling for the arming of black slaves for use in Southern Armies. The Civil War ended less than a month later.

Emancipation Proclamation

On September 22, 1862, President Lincoln issued the Emancipation Proclamation freeing all slaves in territories held by Confederates and emphasized the enlisting of black soldiers in the Union Army. The focus of the Civil War shifted after President Abraham Lincoln signed the Emancipation Proclamation. After that, "freeing the slaves" became a goal for the Union Army.

Slaves held in Texas did not hear news of the Emancipation Proclamation until June 19, 1865 when the Union Army landed in Galveston. Since then, "Juneteenth" has been celebrated by many African Americans.

Civil War Leaders

Abraham Lincoln and Robert E. Lee were two very powerful leaders during the Civil War. They represented very different views of the nature of the United States. With their positions as leaders and their differences in opinion, conflict was bound to happen.

As a Civil War leader, Abraham Lincoln:

- was elected president of the United States in 1860
- opposed the spread of slavery
- issued the Emancipation Proclamation
- was determined to preserve the Union — by force if necessary
- believed the United States was one nation, not a collection of independent states
- wrote the Gettysburg Address that said the Civil War, which began in 1861, was to preserve a government "of the people, by the people, and for the people"

As a Civil War leader, Robert E. Lee:

- was the leader of the Army of Northern Virginia
- was offered the command of the Union forces at the beginning of the war, but chose not to fight against Virginia
- opposed secession, but did not believe the union should be held together by force
- urged Southerners to accept defeat at the end of the war and reunite as Americans when some wanted to continue fighting

Other leaders:

Ulysses S. Grant was general of the Union army that defeated Robert E. Lee and the Confederate Army.

Jefferson Davis was president of the Confederate States of America.

GRANT

DAVIS

Native Americans in the Civil War

North

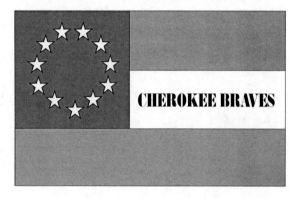

Ely Parker was a Chief of the Six Nations of the Iroquois at the young age of 23. He studied law and wanted to become a lawyer, but he was not considered a citizen and not allowed to be a lawyer. He met Ulysses S. Grant in Galena, Illinois and saved him in a fight. Afterward, he was admitted into the Army and served on General Grant's staff. Because he knew the law and could write very well, Parker was chosen to write Grant's terms for Lee's surrender. At Lee's surrender, Parker was promoted to Brigadier General.

South

Native Americans fought bravely for both the Union and the Confederacy during the Civil War. Indians forced to live on reservations were upset with the United States government and decided to join the Confederacy. Stand Watie, a Cherokee Indian Chief, led Indian troops in more battles west of the Mississippi River than any other unit. Stand Watie was the only Indian General on either side during the war.

CHEROKEE BRAVES

If you were a Native American during the Civil War, would you fight for the North, the South, or remain neutral?

_____

_____

_____

_____

_____

_____

_____

FAST FACT!

Upon meeting Ely Parker, General Lee stated, "I am glad to see one real American," and Parker replied, "We are all Americans."

Gettysburg: July 1–3, 1863

General Robert E. Lee held the small town of Gettysburg, Pennsylvania. He knew that the Union Army was larger and was waiting for Confederate General Longstreet and reinforcements. Fighting continued for three days in and around the town. Eventually, the Union Army was victorious. This battle was a turning point in the war. The Northern victory left the South with no chance of winning the Civil War.

GETTYSBURG STATISTICS

	Killed	Wounded	Captured/Missing
Confederate	3,903	18,735	5,425
Union	3,155	14,529	5,365

Do the Math!

1. How many more Union soldiers were captured or missing after the battle? _____

2. How many more Confederate troops were killed during the battle? _____

3. How many more Confederate troops were wounded? _____

4. How many soldiers were killed altogether? _____

5. How many soldiers were wounded altogether? _____

Gettysburg Address

The Gettysburg Address is a short speech that United States President Abraham Lincoln delivered during the American Civil War at the site of the Battle of Gettysburg in Pennsylvania. He delivered the address on November 19, 1863, at ceremonies to dedicate a part of the battlefield as a cemetery for those who had lost their lives in the battle. Lincoln wrote the final version of the address—the fifth written version—in 1864. This version also differed somewhat from the speech he actually gave, but it was the only copy he signed. It is carved on a stone plaque in the Lincoln Memorial.

Four score and seven years ago our fathers brought forth on this continent, a new nation, conceived in Liberty, and dedicated to the proposition that all men are created equal.

Now we are engaged in a great civil war, testing whether that nation, or any nation so conceived and so dedicated, can long endure. We are met on a great battlefield of that war. We have come to dedicate a portion of that field, as a final resting place for those who here gave their lives that that nation might live. It is altogether fitting and proper that we should do this.

But, in a larger sense, we can not dedicate — we can not consecrate--we can not hallow — this ground. The brave men, living and dead, who struggled here, have consecrated it, far above our poor power to add or detract. The world will little note, nor long remember what we say here, but it can never forget what they did here. It is for us the living, rather, to be dedicated here to the unfinished work which they who fought here have thus far so nobly advanced. It is rather for us to be here dedicated to the great task remaining before us — that from these honored dead we take increased devotion to that cause for which they gave the last full measure of devotion — that we here highly resolve that these dead shall not have died in vain — that this nation, under God, shall have a new birth of freedom — and that government of the people, by the people, for the people, shall not perish from the earth.

FAST FACT!

A "score" is twenty years. How many years is four score and seven years? Which year and event did Lincoln refer to at the beginning of the Gettysburg Address.

The Southern Submarine!

During the Civil War, President Lincoln used the U.S. Navy to blockade Southern ports. The strategy was to keep supplies from reaching Confederates. The South needed a way to break through the blockades. H.L. Hunley, a Southerner, began work on a submarine.

On February 17, 1864, the C.S.S. *Hunley* sank the U.S.S. *Housatonic*. The Hunley became the first submarine to sink another ship. The *Housatonic* sank in about three minutes. The *Hunley* crew signaled Confederates on shore with a blue light. Mysteriously, the *Hunley* sank immediately.

For many years, adventurers searched for the *Hunley* with no luck. Circus showman P.T. Barnum once offered $100,000 for anyone who found and recovered the sunken submarine. Finally in 1995, author Clive Cussler and his National Underwater Marine Agency discovered the submarine under 30 feet of water and about 3 feet of silt near the mouth of Charleston Harbor. On August 8, 2000, the *Hunley* was raised. Research on the *Hunley* continues at the Warren Lasch Conservation Center in Charleston, South Carolina.

Build a Pen Cap Submarine

HERE'S WHAT YOU WILL NEED:
- a pen cap
- modeling clay
- a 2 liter plastic bottle (with cap)

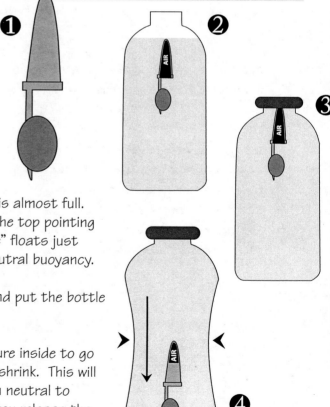

1 Put a ball of clay on the stem of the pen cap.

2 Pour the water into the plastic bottle until it is almost full. Put the pen cap ("submarine") in bottle with the top pointing up. Add or subtract clay until the "submarine" floats just below the surface of the water. It now has neutral buoyancy.

3 Completely fill the plastic bottle with water and put the bottle cap on tightly.

4 Squeeze the bottle. This will cause the pressure inside to go up and the air trapped inside the pen cap will shrink. This will change the buoyancy of your "submarine" from neutral to negative and it will sink to the bottom. When you release the pressure the air will expand and the sub will rise.

Appomattox Court House

The Civil War left a legacy of misery. Thousands of American families buried loved ones. Many soldiers returned home without an arm or leg. Amputation was generally the only "cure" doctors had for battlefield wounds. Other soldiers lost their sight, or suffered from depression or other physical or mental conditions. Croplands and cities were burned. Everyone was dismayed at the extent of the destruction.

On April 9, 1865, General Lee surrendered the Southern forces to Union General Ulysses S. Grant at Appomattox Court House, Virginia. Instead of a joyous victory celebration, most soldiers—on both sides—quietly returned home to recover from the devastation of the war.

Appomattox Court House was a little country settlement in central Virginia. It became a National Historical Park in 1954.

The Civil War lasted for four long years and many lives were lost. **Write down how you think each person felt on April 9, 1865.**

GENERAL LEE _____

_____

GENERAL GRANT _____

_____

THE SOLDIERS _____

_____

THE FAMILIES _____

_____

Additional Web Resources

American Red Cross Museum — www.redcross.org/museum

Antietam (Sharpsburg) — www.nps.gov/anti

Appomattox Court House — www.nps.gov/apco

C.S.S. *Hunley* — www.hunley.org

Fort Sumter — www.nps.gov/fosu

Gettysburg — www.nps.gov/gett

Gettysburg Address — www.loc.gov/exhibits/gadd

Harper's Ferry — www.nps.gov/hafe/home.htm

Manassas (Bull Run) — http://www.nps.gov/mana

Vicksburg — www.nps.gov/vick

Glossary

abolitionist: one who works against slavery; someone who does not agree with slavery; a person who opposes slavery; a person who fought to end slavery

amendment: a correction or change made to a document such as the U.S. Constitution; a change in, or addition to, a constitution, law, or bill

barracks: a building or group of buildings for soldiers to live in, usually in a fort or military camp

confederation: a united league or alliance

democracy: government where people hold the ruling power

free-soil: area where slavery was not allowed

...tyr: person who suffers or dies rather than give up his beliefs

...oclamation: an official public statement

rebellious: fighting against people in charge

secession: when a group of states leaves an established union to start their own country

Answer Key

Page 8: The War between the States
Page 9: 1. N; 2. S; 3. S; 4. S; 5.N
Page 10: 1. Texas, Louisiana, Arkansas, Missouri, Mississippi, Tennessee, Kentucky, Alabama, Georgia, Florida, South Carolina, North Carolina, Virginia, (Slave States); 2. Maine, Massachusetts, New Hampshire, Vermont, Rhode Island, Connecticut, New Jersey, New York, Pennsylvania, Ohio, Indiana, Illinois, Michigan, Wisconsin, Iowa, Minnesota, Kansas, Oregon, and California; 3. 7; 4. 20; 5. 15
Page 11: 1. D; 2. B; 3. C; 4. E; 5. F; 6. H; 7. G; 8. A
Page 14: 1. 1,299; 2. 73; 3. 458
Page 22: 1. 1,247; 2. 592; 3. 525; 4. 4,808; 5. 18,573
Page 26: 1. 60; 2. 748; 3. 4,206; 4. 7,058; 5. 33,264

Index